Appetizing A Recipes

A Complete Cookbook of Middle-Eastern Dish Ideas!

BY

Julia Chiles

Copyright 2019 - Julia Chiles

OOOOOOOOOOOOOOOOOOOOOOOOOOOOOOOOOOOO

License Notes

No part of this Book can be reproduced in any form or by any means including print, electronic, scanning or photocopying unless prior permission is granted by the author.

All ideas, suggestions and guidelines mentioned here are written for informative purposes. While the author has taken every possible step to ensure accuracy, all readers are advised to follow information at their own risk. The author cannot be held responsible for personal and/or commercial damages in case of misinterpreting and misunderstanding any part of this Book

OOOOOOOOOOOOOOOOOOOOOOOOOOOOOOOO

Thanks for Purchasing My Book! - Here's Your Reward!

Thank you so much for purchasing my book! As a reward for your purchase, you can now receive free books sent to you every week. All you have to do is just subscribe to the list by entering your email address in the box below and I will send you a notification every time I have a free promotion running. The books will absolutely be free with no work at all from you! Who doesn't want free books? No one! *There are free and discounted books every day*, and an email is sent to you 1-2 days beforehand to remind you so you don't miss out. It's that easy! Enter your email now to get started!

∽ **Sign up now & get your free e-book** ∾   Refreshing recepies

FIRST NAME: John
YOUR EMAIL: username@domain.com

SIGN UP

http://julia-chiles.subscribemenow.com

OOOOOOOOOOOOOOOOOOOOOOOOOOOOOOOOOO

Table of Contents

Introduction 7

1 – Albanian Mixed Vegetables 9

2 – White Bean Soup 11

3 – Fried Meatballs 14

4 – Albanian Sausages 17

5 – Albanian Chicken Soup 19

6 – Lamb and Okra Stew 22

7 – Leek Casserole 25

8 – Stuffed Vine Leaves 27

9 – Veal and Walnuts 31

10 – Lamb Pasta Soup 34

11 – Baked Lamb with Yogurt 37

12 – Beet Root Pie 40

13 – Albanian Stuffed Peppers 44

14 – Albanian Salami and Chicken 48

15 – Albanian-Style Vegetable Pie 51

16 – Spinach, Eggs and Rice 54

17 – Albanian Cucumber and Tomato Salad 57

18 – Albanian Eggplant, Peppers and Zucchini 59

19 – Baked Tuna and Garlic 62

20 – Lemon and Egg Soup 64

21 – Cabbage Stew 66

22 – Rabbit Casserole 69

23 – Baked Lamb and Rice 72

24 – Veal and Lima Beans 76

25 – Albanian Musaka 79

Delectable Albanian Dessert Recipes… 82

26 – Ravani 83

27 – Albanian-Style Rice Pudding 86

28 – Stuffed Figs 88

29 – Albanian Sheqerpare 90

30 – Honey Baklava 94

Conclusion 98

Author's Afterthoughts 100

About the Author 101

ooooooooooooooooooooooooooooooooo

Introduction

Are you tired of preparing the same types of recipes all the time? Looking for a type of cuisine that is a little more interesting?

Albanians use many foods common to the Mediterranean basin in their delectable cuisine. They include vegetables, fruits, fish, dairy products, wheat and olives. They grow citrus fruits, and figs are a great favorite, too.

Nearly everyone breaks for lunch in Albania, from children in school to government and public workers. It's the meal of the day when families are most often found together, sharing time and good food.

When speaking about regional foods, you can almost divide Albania into three separate regions. In northern areas of the country, corn is used often, in breads and mealtime dishes both salty and sweet. They also have many types of fresh fruits and vegetables, with a good climate.

In the central region, they can grow most any crop they please. They also use turkey, chicken, goose and duck in many dishes. Fish like sole, mullet and perch are caught in the nearby Adriatic Sea.

In Southern Albania, they raise most of the nation's cattle, and they serve more dairy products than their neighbors. Throughout the country, there are many taste temptations and you'll enjoy preparing them in your own home.

OOOOOOOOOOOOOOOOOOOOOOOOOOOOOOOOOOOO

1 - Albanian Mixed Vegetables

Vegetable dishes are varied and interesting in Albanian cuisine. They are a refreshing, light accompaniment to meat dishes. Italian cuisine's influence shows up here in the use of vegetables.

Serving Size: 4 Servings

Total Cooking Time: 45-55 minutes

Ingredients:

- 2 pounds of your favorite veggies, like potatoes, zucchini, eggplant, peppers, etc.
- 1/2 cup of oil, olive
- 1 cup of onions, chopped
- 1 cup of tomatoes, peeled and chopped
- 1 tbsp. of parsley, chopped, as desired
- Salt, kosher, as desired
- Pepper, ground, as desired

Instructions:

1. Cut off any inedible vegetable tips. Wash the veggies well and cut into 1" squares.

2. Sauté the vegetables in 1/2 of your oil in fry pan. Remove them. Sauté tomatoes and onions in remaining oil. Season as desired.

3. Place all ingredients in stock pot with 1 cup water. Cover. Simmer till the moisture has almost all cooked away. Serve hot.

OOOOOOOOOOOOOOOOOOOOOOOOOOOOOOOOO

2 - White Bean Soup

This soup will surprise you with its taste, since its ingredients are so simple. You can use canned beans if you don't feel like soaking bagged beans overnight.

Serving Size: 5 Servings

Total Cooking Time: 4 & 1/4 hours + 12 hours sitting time

Ingredients:

- 1 & 1/2 cups of white beans, dry, washed and picked over, soaked overnight, then rinsed
- 4 cups of water, filtered
- 1 medium onion, chopped
- 1/4 cup of butter, unsalted
- 3 tbsp. of tomato paste, no salt added
- 1/4 cup of chopped parsley, flat leaf
- 1 tbsp. of paprika, sweet
- Salt, sea, as desired
- 1/2 tsp. of chili powder, as desired

Instructions:

1. Add water and pre-soaked beans to large sized pot. Bring to boil. Cook for 8-10 minutes.

2. Add onion and butter to skillet over med. heat. Cook till they are tender and add then to beans.

3. Add chili powder, as desired, along with paprika, parsley and tomato paste. Combine well. Lower heat to simmer. Cover. Cook for three to four hours. Add additional water, as needed. Season to taste.

4. For optimum taste, cover the soup and let it sit in the fridge for one to two days. This particular soup benefits a great deal from the sitting time. Serve.

OOOOOOOOOOOOOOOOOOOOOOOOOOOOOOOOO

3 – Fried Meatballs

Meatballs in Albania are generally made with either lamb, beef or chicken. This recipe uses beef. They are often fried, as these are, and the addition of mint at the end gives them a unique taste.

Serving Size: 4 Servings

Total Cooking Time: 40 minutes

Ingredients:

- 1 pound of beef (or other meat), ground
- 1 slice of bread, stale
- 1 grated onion, small
- 2 tbsp. of chopped cheese, feta
- 2 tbsp. of breadcrumbs
- 2 tbsp. of butter, melted or oil
- 1 tbsp. of parsley, chopped
- 1 cup of flour, all-purpose
- 1 cup of oil, olive
- As desired:
- Salt, kosher
- Pepper, ground
- Oregano
- Mint

Instructions:

1. Soak stale bread in filtered water. Drain by squeezing hard.

2. Add the ground beef, mint, salt, pepper, parsley, onion, butter or oil and breadcrumbs to large bowl.

3. Mix well. Form into patties of 1" thickness. Season as desired. Roll patties in flour. Fry them in hot oil. Serve with mashed potatoes or French Fries.

OOOOOOOOOOOOOOOOOOOOOOOOOOOOOOOO

4 – Albanian Sausages

Cevapcici, or Albanian sausages, are tasty homemade Balkan meats that do vary from one area to another. The main ingredients are the same, and some add onion and spices, while others do not.

Serving Size: 3 Servings

Total Cooking Time: 20 minutes

Ingredients:

- 1 & 1/3 lbs. of young beef, ground
- Salt, kosher
- Pepper, ground, black
- Several leaves of rosemary
- 3 & 1/3 fluid ounces of oil, olive

Instructions:

1. Chop or grind ingredients finely.

2. Work ingredients into mixture with meat.

3. Chill for 1-2 hours in fridge.

4. Form into link-shaped sausages. Turn while grilling them and brush with oil. Serve with onions.

OOOOOOOOOOOOOOOOOOOOOOOOOOOOOOOOOO

5 - Albanian Chicken Soup

This is among the favorite soups of cooks in Albania. They enjoy making it, as well as eating it. It's quite easy and does not require many ingredients. It tastes especially good on chilly spring or cold winter days.

Serving Size: 2-3 Servings

Total Cooking Time: 1 hour & 10 minutes

Ingredients:

- Chicken breasts
- 3-4 tomatoes, medium
- 1 onion, large
- 2 cloves of garlic
- 1 handful rice
- Filtered water
- Olive oil

Instructions:

1. Boil water in a kettle. Start this ahead of time, since you'll need it soon. Chop the onions and garlic. Sauté with a bit of olive oil.

2. As onions, sauté, dice tomatoes. Set them aside. Dice chicken. Add to onions. Allow the chicken to sauté for five minutes with onion. Add tomatoes.

3. Mix well. Add water. Fill pot to top with water. Season as desired. Do not add any more water.

4. When soup boils, lower heat. Allow it to simmer for 15 to 20 minutes. This gives the flavors a chance to meld together and gives the chicken adequate cooking time.

5. Add one handful rice. Don't add too much or you'll have rice soup.

6. Taste soup. Adjust seasoning as desired. Makesure chicken has cooked fully. Remove from heat. Allow to cool just a bit and serve.

ooooooooooooooooooooooooooooooooooo

6 - Lamb and Okra Stew

This Albanian stew doesn't take long to make, and as it cooks, the aroma will amaze you. The okra should be soft, yet not gooey. Don't pierce holes in the okra, since that may make them slimy.

Serving Size: 2 Servings

Total Cooking Time: 40 minutes

Ingredients:

- 8 & 3/4 oz. of okra
- 14 oz. of lamb, diced
- 1 onion, diced
- 2 garlic cloves
- 17 fluid oz. of stock, lamb
- 2 tbsp. of pureed tomatoes
- Oil, olive
- Salt, kosher
- Pepper, black, ground

Instructions:

1. Boil lamb in lightly salted water over high heat for two hours. Drain water through sieve into jug, separating stock and meat.

2. Cut stalk tips from okra. Do not allow any holes to show up. Wash okra in cold water and pat dry. Lay them on baking sheet, spaced out well.

3. Place baking sheet in 300F oven for eight to 10 minutes.

4. As okra bakes, fry onions in oil for several minutes. Add lamb. Brown.

5. Add salt, ground pepper, tomato puree, garlic and 1/2 stock. Combine and simmer for a few minutes.

6. Remove okra from oven. Add to pan with rest of stock. Cover. Simmer for 15-20 minutes.

7. Remove from heat. Allow to stand for a few minutes and serve.

OOOOOOOOOOOOOOOOOOOOOOOOOOOOOOOOO

7 - Leek Casserole

The leek is underused in many Western recipes, more for soups and seasonings than as the base for specific dishes. This recipe proves that the leeks can star in a dish and make it very tasty.

Serving Size: 4 Servings

Total Cooking Time: 1 & 3/4 hour

Ingredients:

- 2 pounds of leeks
- 1/2 cup of oil, olive
- 3/4 cup of onion, chopped
- 1/2 pound of meat, ground
- 1 tbsp. of tomato sauce, no salt added
- Red pepper, mild
- Salt, sea
- Pepper, ground

Instructions:

1. Cut green leaves off leeks. Wash leeks and cut them slantways in slices with 1" thickness.

2. Sauté leeks in a bit of oil. Place in baking pan. Sauté the ground meat and onion in the remaining oil.

3. Add the tomato sauce, beef stock, red pepper, sea salt and ground pepper. Bring mixture to boil.

4. Pour the meat mixture over leeks. Bake for an hour in 375F oven and serve hot.

ooooooooooooooooooooooooooooooooooooo

8 - Stuffed Vine Leaves

Stuffed leaves remind Albanian cooks of summer recipes, and this is a favorite summer dish in Albania. The rolled vine leaves are refreshing, stuffed as they are with minced meat, along with rice, onions, seasonings and herbs.

Serving Size: 32 rolls

Total Cooking Time: 2 hours & 10 minutes

Ingredients:

- 1 & 1/3 ounce of grape leaves, pickled
- 14 ounces of minced lamb
- 5 onions, diced
- 2 & 1/2 ounces of rice
- 1 tsp. of pepper, black, ground
- 1 tsp. of paprika
- 1 tsp. of vegetable stock, dried
- 3/4 ounce of parsley, chopped
- 1 tsp. of basil, fresh
- Oil, olive
- Salt, kosher, as desired
- 2 quarts of filtered water, boiling

Instructions:

1. Add onions to sauté pan. Fry for three to five minutes in oil till onions begin browning.

2. Turn heat off. Add rice, meat, stock, parsley, basil, paprika and pepper. Mix well.

3. Unwrap vine leaves carefully. Place a vine leaf on one hand, with base at palm and tip pointing towards top.

4. Add another vine leaf with tip pointing downward. Overlap well.

5. Place spoonful of rice and meat mixture in middle of leaves. Fold bottom of leaves over mixture. Fold sides in. Roll leaf up and seal the filling in a shape like a parcel.

6. Make a layer of the vine leaves in bottom of deep sauce pan. Add vine leaf rolled parcel on the top.

7. Make as many of these as your rice and meat mixture can make. Add them all to sauce pan. Pack side by side till you cover bottom of sauce pan. Start the next layer atop the first.

8. Pour boiling water sufficient to cover vine leaf tops into sauce pan. Bring to boil. Cover. Allow to simmer for an hour and a half. The water should all be absorbed. If this happens too early, you can add extra water.

9. Remove vine leaf parcels from sauce pan. Allow them to cook for eight to 10 minutes. Serve.

OOOOOOOOOOOOOOOOOOOOOOOOOOOOOOOOO

9 – Veal and Walnuts

This is a simple veal dish from Albania. The walnuts add a wonderful nutty texture and flavor to the recipe. This one is made with veal, but chicken is also used, since many Albanian people raise their own fowl.

Serving Size: 4 Servings

Total Cooking Time: 50-60 minutes

Ingredients:

- 2 tbsp. of flour, all-purpose
- 15 walnuts, shelled, crushed finely
- 2 egg yolks, beaten
- 1 clove of garlic, minced
- 1/4 lb. of butter, unsalted
- 2 to 3 pounds of 1-inch cubed veal

Instructions:

1. Place veal in sauce pan. Cook on med. heat till tender. Remove meat and set aside in dish. Leave the rest of the juices in sauce pan.

2. In separate sauce pan, add flour. Sauté on low till color is light brown. Don't over-cook it.

3. Add 1/8 lb. butter. Add garlic, egg yolks and crushed walnuts and stir well.

4. Add juices from other sauce pan. Sauté till ingredients thicken. Remove immediately from heat so egg yolks don't solidify.

5. Fold in meat. Pan fry the rest of the butter till brown. Pour over individual servings and serve.

ooooooooooooooooooooooooooooooooo

10 - Lamb Pasta Soup

This dish is known as Supë me Mish in Albania. It includes lamb, onions, soup pasta and carrots. They are simmered in a light and tasty sauce made with tomato puree and meat juices.

Serving Size: 4 Servings

Total Cooking Time: 3 & 1/4 hours

Ingredients:

- 7 oz. of pasta
- 7 oz. of lamb
- 2 carrots, diced
- 2 tbsp. of tomato puree, no salt added
- 1 onion, diced
- 2 tbsp. of vegetable stock, dried
- Salt, kosher
- Pepper, ground
- 2 tsp. of parsley, fresh
- Filtered water, boiling
- Oil, olive

Instructions:

1. Place boned lamb in pan of lightly salted boiling water. Bring water back to boil. Cook for about two hours. Meat should be tender.

2. When meat has been prepared, remove it from heat. Remove meat from bones and replace in pan of water. Discard bones. To boil, you'll need about 67 fluid ounces of water, but don't add it all in unless you need it.

3. Fry onion for several minutes in fry pan. Add puree, carrots and 3 & 1/3 fluid ounces of boiling hot water. Allow to simmer for about 10 minutes.

4. Add this mixture into lamb and water pan. Bring back to boil. Allow to simmer for 1/2 hour. Season as desired.

5. Add pasta. Let the mixture simmer for 30 more minutes. Allow to cool just a bit and serve the soup warm.

OOOOOOOOOOOOOOOOOOOOOOOOOOOOOOOOOOO

11 – Baked Lamb with Yogurt

Wintertime is the time of year when this dish is served the most in Albania. Generations gather to fight off the cold by sharing this soup together. It uses lamb, as many Mediterranean recipes do.

Serving Size: 4 Servings

Total Cooking Time: 1 hour & 40 minutes

Ingredients:

- 1 & 1/2 pounds of lamb meat
- 4 tbsp. of butter, unsalted
- 2 tbsp. of rice
- Salt, sea
- Pepper, ground
- For the yogurt sauce
- 1 tbsp. of flour, all-purpose
- 4 tbsp. of butter, unsalted
- 2 pounds of yogurt
- 5 eggs, large
- Salt, sea
- Pepper, ground

Instructions:

1. Cut the lamb in four pieces. Sprinkle them with sea salt and ground pepper. Bake in moderate heat in oven with 1/2 butter. Sprinkle lamb with its own gravy occasionally.

2. When lamb has baked halfway, add the rice. Remove baking pan from oven. Set it aside as you're preparing the sauce.

3. To create sauce, sauté flour in the butter till mixed well. Mix the yogurt with eggs, sea salt and ground pepper till you have a uniform consistency in the mixture. Stir in flour.

4. Put sauce in baking dish. Sauté with lamb pieces. Bake in 375F oven for 40-45 minutes and serve hot.

ooooooooooooooooooooooooooooooooooo

12 – Beet Root Pie

These deep-colored, amazing beet roots are complimented in this recipe with herbs and feta cheese. The pie offers flavor as well as good nutrition, and the taste is slightly sweet.

Serving Size: 12 slices

Total Cooking Time: 1 & 3/4 hour

Ingredients:

- 8 filo pastry sheets, pre-packaged
- 5 beet roots, diced
- 5 eggs, large
- 1 & 3/4 oz. of basil, chopped
- 1 & 3/4 oz. of parsley, chopped
- 3 & 1/2 oz. of Feta cheese, crumbled
- 3 & 1/2 oz. of spinach, chopped
- 1 onion, grated
- 1 tsp. of pepper, ground
- Oil, olive
- 7 & 1/2 fluid oz. of water, filtered

Instructions:

1. Wash beet root and trim stalks down. Place in sauce pan. Cover it with filtered water. Bring to boil till it softens. This usually takes 35-40 minutes.

2. After beet root has cooked, drain and allow to cool for 1/2 hour. Wear gloves to rub beet root skin gently away. Dice into chunks. Place in large sized bowl.

3. To create the filling, add onion, ground pepper, cheese, spinach, basil, parsley and eggs to beet root. Mix well.

4. Layer the sheets of pre-made filo pastry atop each other. Brush olive oil between them as you're laying them down. Once six of the eight sheets have been laid, add beet root filling over the top.

5. Repeat layering till you have six of eight sheets atop filling. Each should be brushed with olive oil. Brush on thin oil layer over top.

6. Bake in 350F oven for an hour, or till they are a golden brown in color. Remove.

7. Pour 1/2 cup filtered water over top. Pour 1/2 cup water around edges. Cover with two small tea towels. Allow to set for an hour. Serve.

OOOOOOOOOOOOOOOOOOOOOOOOOOOOOOOOOO

13 - Albanian Stuffed Peppers

These stuffed peppers are prepared in a way that is somewhat unique to Albania. The stuffing includes ground meat, rice, tomatoes, parsley and onions. The taste will blow you away.

Serving Size: 5 Servings

Total Cooking Time: 2 hours & 45 minutes

Ingredients:

- 10 peppers, mild
- 1 pound of beef, ground
- 2 onions, medium
- 1 cup of chopped parsley, fresh
- 1 tbsp. of salt, sea
- 1/2 tsp. of pepper, ground
- 1 cup of uncooked rice
- Optional: 2 baking potatoes, medium
- 2 tbsp. of oil, olive
- 1 x 14 to 16 ounce can of tomatoes, crushed
- 3 cups of water, filtered

Instructions:

1. Wash and clean peppers. Remove seeds and pat peppers dry. You can keep the top part so it will serve as decoration atop stuffing.

2. Chop onions and sauté them on oil on med-high heat. Add ground beef. After meat has browned, add crushed tomatoes and parsley. Add a cup of filtered water. Combine fully.

3. When mixture begins boiling, add rice, sea salt and ground pepper. Reduce heat to med. Combine well. Allow mixture to cook for eight to 10 minutes. The stuffing should not be overly thick. You can add 1/2 cup more water if you need it.

4. Turn off heat. Allow stuffing to begin cooling. While still a bit warm, stuff peppers and place on baking dish.

5. After peppers have been stuffed, cut potatoes. Place around peppers. They help to absorb excess water, later in the process.

6. After peppers are stuffed, you will generally have some leftover stuffing. You may have a bit less stuffing if the peppers are big. Just make them look as good as they can. Any extra stuffing can be added around peppers, on top of potatoes. Salt potatoes, as well. Add two cups of filtered water around peppers & potatoes.

7. Bake in 375F oven for 30-35 minutes. If tops of peppers are browning but potatoes aren't baked fully yet, cover baking dish with foil. Allow to bake for 15 additional minutes. Allow dish to cool a bit before serving.

OOOOOOOOOOOOOOOOOOOOOOOOOOOOOOOOOO

14 - Albanian Salami and Chicken

The native-made salami of Albania gives dishes extra texture and natural spices. You can mix it with plain casseroles, or use it with chicken, as this recipe does.

Serving Size: 4 Servings

Total Cooking Time: 1 & 1/4 hour

Ingredients:

- 12 drumsticks, chicken
- 1 diced onion, red
- 1 diced onion, yellow
- 4-inch Albanian salami, sliced
- 1 tbsp. of rosemary, fresh
- Pepper, ground
- Oil, olive

Instructions:

1. Add small sized drizzle of oil on bottom of flat baking dish. Ceramic dishes work well to keep ingredients from sticking.

2. Add chicken and onions to baking dish. Season using rosemary and ground pepper. Add salami slices carefully between drumsticks. Don't place against sides of dish or they could burn.

3. Drizzle oil over top of dish.

4. Cook in 350F oven for about an hour. Turn chicken after 1/2 hour. Remove from oven and allow to sit for a few minutes. Serve hot.

OOOOOOOOOOOOOOOOOOOOOOOOOOOOOOOO

15 – Albanian-Style Vegetable Pie

This vegetable pie recipe is a great way to take your cooking back to the basics. The pastry leaves are sometimes rolled at home, or, as with this recipe, purchased as filo dough slices.

Serving Size: 4-6 Servings

Total Cooking Time: 50 minutes

Ingredients:

- 1 cup of oil, olive
- 30 slices of filo pastry dough
- 1 & 1/2 pounds of chopped spinach, fresh
- 1 cup of feta cheese, diced
- 1/2 cup of green onion, chopped
- 2 or 3 eggs, large
- 1 & 1/2 tsp. of salt, kosher

Instructions:

1. Brush medium, round baking pan with some olive oil.

2. Begin laying slices of pastry inside pan. They should overlap pan edges by an inch or so.

3. Lay two slices down. Brush or sprinkle with olive oil. Lay two more. Repeat process till you have used half of dough slices.

4. Add eggs, onions, oil and feta cheese. Spread mixture on pastry slices.

5. Cover spinach with remainder of pastry slices by repeating the steps used in laying the first slices down.

6. Roll hanging edges of bottom slices over top of pie. Sprinkle with olive oil.

7. Bake in 350F oven for 40-45 minutes, till golden brown in color. Serve hot.

OOOOOOOOOOOOOOOOOOOOOOOOOOOOOOOOOO

16 – Spinach, Eggs and Rice

Albanian Buryani – so simple yet so tasty. It's easily made, healthy and inexpensive. Basmati rice is quite flavorful when cooked with eggs and spinach.

Serving Size: 6 Servings

Total Cooking Time: 1/2 hour

Ingredients:

- 3/4 lb. of spinach, fresh
- 1 & 1/2 oz. of rice
- 1 onion, diced
- 1 tsp. of basil, fresh
- 6 eggs, large
- 3/4 oz. of butter, unsalted
- Salt, kosher
- Pepper, ground
- 1 tbsp. of oil, olive
- 1 quart of filtered water, boiling

Instructions:

1. In large sized sauce pan, melt oil and butter together. While they are melting, fill a kettle with one ounce of filtered water. Bring to boil.

2. Add onion to oil and butter in pan. Fry for several minutes till butter has melted fully and onion is beginning to turn brown.

3. Add rice. Stir constantly for one minute to mix rice with onion. Add boiling water carefully – it may spit. Cover pan. Bring to boil. Leave pan sitting for 8-10 minutes.

4. Add spinach. Stir till wilted completely. Bring mixture back to boil. Allow to boil uncovered till you only have a bit of liquid remaining on bottom of pan.

5. Crack eggs over top of mixture – now called Buryani. Cover with lid. Only allow the eggs to cook for a few minutes. Make sure whites have cooked fully before you remove from heat. Set pan aside to cool for three to five minutes and serve.

OOOOOOOOOOOOOOOOOOOOOOOOOOOOOOOOOO

17 - Albanian Cucumber and Tomato Salad

This colorful, tasty salad **Serving Size:** an excellent first course or side dish for a meal. You can add more salt and ground pepper if you like, and perhaps fresh herbs and fresh squeezed lemon juice.

Serving Size: 4 Servings

Total Cooking Time: 20 minutes

Ingredients:

- 2 or 3 diced tomatoes
- 1 quartered, sliced cucumber
- 1 sliced onion, small
- 1 diced pepper, green
- 1/8 cup of oil, olive
- 1/2 cup of cheese, feta
- 1/2 cup of olives, kalamata

Instructions:

1. Combine peppers, onion, cucumber and tomatoes in medium bowl. Toss well.

2. Drizzle oil over salad. Season as desired. Garnish with cheese and olives. Serve.

ooooooooooooooooooooooooooooooooooo

18 - Albanian Eggplant, Peppers and Zucchini

There are quite a few variations of this recipe, and similar recipes are found in Bulgaria, Turkey, Macedonia and Serbia. It is quite tasty as a side dish, or you can mix it with pasta for a filling meal.

Serving Size: various number of servings

Total Cooking Time: 1 & 1/2 hour

Ingredients:

- 2 & 3/4 pounds of eggplants
- 3 & 1/3 pounds of zucchini
- 1 piece of chopped cucumber
- 1/2 pound of yogurt
- 2 tbsp. of salt, sea
- 4 garlic cloves

Instructions:

1. Peel eggplants lengthways in strips, then into long slices. Sprinkle with salt. Place in lightly salted water for 30 minutes so they can be drained of bitter juice.

2. Squeeze eggplants individually before placing in hot oil. Fry on both sides and drain excess oil away. Place on serving plate.

3. Scrape zucchini skin till you can see the green parts. Use salt to sprinkle and set aside for an hour and a half.

4. Put water and flour together in medium bowl. Mix well.

5. Place zucchini in the water and flour mixture, then in hot oil. Fry till golden on both sides. Place with peppers and eggplants.

6. Mix yogurt and cucumber and pour this over fried veggies. Serve.

ooooooooooooooooooooooooooooooooooo

19 - Baked Tuna and Garlic

This tuna recipe as almost as healthy as it is delicious. It is seasoned in a simple way, with stock, garlic and tomatoes. Fish dishes are popular in the coastal areas of Albania.

Serving Size: 2 Servings

Total Cooking Time: 35 minutes

Ingredients:

- 2 steaks, tuna
- 1 large tomato, sliced
- 1 sliced garlic clove
- 1 tbsp. of stock, vegetable
- 1/3 oz. of parsley, chopped finely
- Salt, kosher
- Pepper, ground
- Oil, olive

Instructions:

1. To prepare base for fish, layer tomato on bottom of baking dish. Place a couple garlic slices on the top of the tomatoes. Sprinkle using dried veggie stock.

2. Lightly brush fish with oil. Place atop tomatoes. Add more sliced garlic. Drizzle with a little more oil on top. Season as desired. Add parsley.

3. Bake tuna dish in 350F oven for 20-25 minutes. Tuna should begin flaking when it is done. It can be eaten while a bit of pink remains in middle. Serve.

oooooooooooooooooooooooooooooooooooo

20 - Lemon and Egg Soup

This is a popular Albanian soup, especially in the winter, with the wind howling outside. Some people make it with chicken. It is a natural comfort food, loved by many.

Serving Size: 4 Servings

Total Cooking Time: 45 minutes

Ingredients:

- 1 & 3/4 liquid pints of broth, chicken
- 4 eggs, large
- 2 lemons, fresh squeezed
- 3 tbsp. of butter, unsalted
- 3 tbsp. of flour, all-purpose
- Salt, sea
- Pepper, WHITE
- Parsley, fresh

Instructions:

1. Melt the butter in medium pot. Add flour and make roux. Add the broth. Simmer for 8-10 minutes.

2. Beat the eggs in large sized bowl. Add lemon juice. Use sea salt and white pepper to season.

3. Remove broth from heat. Stir constantly while adding it to bowl of eggs and lemon. Pour soup through sieve. Place over low heat for a minute and stir constantly again. Garnish with parsley and serve.

OOOOOOOOOOOOOOOOOOOOOOOOOOOOOOOOOOO

21 - Cabbage Stew

Mish me lakra, the Albanian name for this dish, literally means meat and cabbage. Use small sized pieces of meat and choose from lamb or beef. You can use more or less meat in the stew or go meatless.

Serving Size: 4 Servings

Total Cooking Time: 2 & 3/4 hours

Ingredients:

- 1 head of cabbage
- 1 pound of meat, stew
- 1 onion, medium
- 2 tsp. of paprika, sweet
- 2 to 3 heaping tsp. of tomato paste, no salt added
- 2 to 3 heaping tsp. of pepper paste, red
- Salt, sea
- Oil, olive
- 1/4 tsp. of chili flakes, red
- 1 bay leaf, dried

Instructions:

1. Add the stew meat and a bit of oil into pot. Cover and allow to cook. This will allow meat to become its most tender. Cook for 1/2 hour or longer, checking on it periodically.

2. Peel outer cabbage leaves. Discard. Remove the core and discard it, too. Slice cabbage into cubes that are roughly bite sized. Rinse the cabbage well.

3. Chop onion. Add to meat pot. Add oil, tomato and pepper paste. Add chili flakes and paprika. Stir well. When you can smell the aroma from pepper flakes, add cabbage. Add water to cover it. Add the bay leaf.

4. Bring stew to boil. Season as desired. Simmer till cabbage has cooked. Cook stew over med-low heat. It will take two hours or so for cabbage and meat to become tender. Remove and discard the bay leaf. Serve with fresh bread.

OOOOOOOOOOOOOOOOOOOOOOOOOOOOOOOO

22 – Rabbit Casserole

It's difficult to find really good rabbit dishes, but this entry is delicious and unique. It comes from the Adriatic region of Croatia and Albania. It includes garlic, tomatoes and olive oil to give it an appealing taste.

Serving Size: 1-2 Servings

Total Cooking Time: 2 & 1/2 hours + 8 hours marinating time

Ingredients:

- 1 jointed rabbit
- 4 or 5 chopped tomatoes, fresh
- 2 bay leaves
- 5 fluid oz. of oil, olive
- 4 tbsp. of vinegar, red wine
- 1/4 tsp. of sugar, granulated
- 4 peeled garlic cloves
- 10 fluid ounces of filtered water, hot
- 1 small cinnamon stick piece
- Salt, kosher
- Pepper, black, ground
- 1 & 1/2 pounds of whole, peeled onions, small
- 1 rosemary sprig
- 1 glass red wine, small

Instructions:

1. Rinse pieces of rabbit. Place in large bowl with bay leaves. Sprinkle vinegar over pieces. Allow to marinate overnight in refrigerator.

2. Heat 1/2 of oil in sauce pan. Pat pieces of rabbit dry. Fry in oil till browned well over both sides. Remove. Put on plate.

3. When all pieces of rabbit are fried, place back in sauce pan with wine, rosemary, spices, bay leaves and garlic cloves.

4. Add tomatoes, hot water and sugar. Season as desired. Cover pan. Cook for an hour or so.

5. Heat remaining oil in fry pan. Fry onions gently. Stir occasionally till they are a golden color.

6. Add fry pan contents to sauce pan. Shake to spread onions evenly. Cover pan. Simmer for 15 more minutes. Serve.

OOOOOOOOOOOOOOOOOOOOOOOOOOOOOOOOOO

23 - Baked Lamb and Rice

Here we have come to Albania's national dish. It doesn't sound like anything spectacular, just looking at the ingredients, but it is very tasty, and the same type of dish as the favorite Middle-Eastern moussaka.

Serving Size: 8 Servings

Total Cooking Time: 2 hours & 10 minutes

Ingredients:

- 2 & 1/2 ounces of butter, unsalted
- 1 tbsp. of oil, olive
- 2 & 1/2 lbs. of cubed lamb shoulder, boned
- 4 grated cloves of garlic
- 1 tsp. of oregano, dried
- 2 & 1/4 ounces of rinsed rice, long-grain
- 1 & 3/4 ounces of flour, plain
- 20 fluid ounces of yogurt, Greek style
- 4 beaten eggs, large
- To garnish: nutmeg, fresh grated
- Salt, kosher
- Pepper, black, ground

Instructions:

1. Preheat oven to 350F.

2. Heat 3/4 ounces of butter plus oil in large covered pan on high heat, Brown lamb. You can do this in batches.

3. Return all lamb together to pan. Add 7 fluid ounces of water, along with garlic and oregano. Bring to simmer. Cover and cook for 50-60 minutes, till lamb has become tender.

4. Add rice. Season as desired. Transfer mixture to 5-pint baking dish.

5. Melt the rest of the butter in small sized sauce pan. Add flour. Make roux. Cook for just a couple minutes and remove from heat.

6. Add yogurt. Combine fully and return to heat. Gently cook for two minutes or so. Remove from heat. Add in beaten eggs. Season as desired.

7. Pour sauce over rice and lamb mixture. Grate nutmeg over the top. Bake for 35-45 minutes till it starts turning a golden brown in color. Remove from oven. Leave sitting for about five minutes and then serve.

ooooooooooooooooooooooooooooooooo

24 – Veal and Lima Beans

This is a genuine Albanian dish, and like the country itself, you'll find that it is quite down to earth. It's a filling meal and perfect for dinner with your family, even on a weeknight.

Serving Size: 2-4 Servings

Total Cooking Time: 1 hour & 5 minutes

Ingredients:

- 1 & 1/2 pounds of veal
- 1 grated onion, large
- 1 & 1/2 pounds of Lima beans, large
- Salt, kosher
- Pepper, ground
- Tomatoes, ripe

Instructions:

1. Cube the veal shoulder parts. Wash meat well using cold water and drain the cubes. Place in pot with grated onions and butter. Stir-fry for several minutes.

2. As meat fries, add water till it covers all pieces. Season as desired and add 2-3 tbsp. of tomatoes. Cover pot. Allow mixture to boil.

3. Remove ends from Lima beans. Clean well. Halve if desired. Add to meat. Add water to cover all pot ingredients.

4. When beans have finished boiling, add remainder of tomatoes. Allow stew to boil for several more minutes, thickening the liquid. Serve.

OOOOOOOOOOOOOOOOOOOOOOOOOOOOOOOOOO

25 - Albanian Musaka

This dish is somewhat similar to Greek Moussaka, but it uses potatoes, rather than eggplant. The sliced potatoes are layered with meat, and covered in sauce, before being baked. It's another Albanian comfort food.

Serving Size: 8 Servings

Total Cooking Time: 1 & 3/4 hour

Ingredients:

- 8-10 washed, peeled, thinly sliced potatoes, fried with butter
- 6 eggs, large
- 1 & 1/2 pound of beef, ground
- 3 simmered onions, medium
- 1 tsp. of oregano
- 1 tsp. of paprika
- Salt, sea
- Pepper, ground
- 1 quart of scalded milk, whole

Instructions:

1. Fry the hamburger and mix the burger ingredients.

2. Arrange one layer of potato slices on the bottom of a 9x15" baking dish. Top with one layer of the hamburger mixture.

3. Add another layer of potatoes, then hamburger mixture. Repeat and finish the top layer with potato slices.

4. Slowly mix beaten eggs with scalded milk.

5. Pour milk and egg mixture over baking dish, barely covering the top layer.

6. Bake in 350F oven for an hour. Serve hot.

oooooooooooooooooooooooooooooooooo

Delectable Albanian Dessert Recipes...

ooooooooooooooooooooooooooooooooo

26 - Ravani

Ravani is somewhat similar to sponge cake served in Great Britain, but the yogurt **Serving Size:** the texture of this cake denser. It is eaten mainly as a cold dessert, but sometimes as a sweet breakfast, too.

Serving Size: 12 Servings

Total Cooking Time: 1 & 1/4 hour

Ingredients:

- 1 tsp. of baking soda
- 3 & 3/4 ounces of yogurt, Greek
- 15 & 1/2 ounces of sugar, granulated
- 2 eggs, large
- 5 & 1/3 ounces of flour, all-purpose
- Oil, olive

Instructions:

1. Pour eggs and sugar into large bowl. Add baking soda and yogurt. The yogurt activates the baking soda.

2. Add a couple handfuls of flour to the bowl. Mix and continue adding flour till mixture is thickened.

3. Use a 2-inch deep large sized baking dish and grease with oil. Pour mixture into it. Bang tray down a few times so the mixture is flat.

4. Place Ravani in cold oven. Turn oven to 350F. Cook for 40-45 minutes till the Ravani is golden brown.

5. Turn off oven. Leave cake inside. Leave door of oven open for 15-20 minutes.

6. Remove Ravani from oven. Slice into squares or diamonds. Place on serving platter. Serve.

OOOOOOOOOOOOOOOOOOOOOOOOOOOOOOOOOOOO

27 - Albanian-Style Rice Pudding

This recipe was already easy, and now it uses a slow cooker, so it's even simpler. It tends to thicken up a bit more in the slow cooker, so be sure you use enough milk.

Serving Size: 4 Servings

Total Cooking Time: 5 minutes + 3-4 hours slow cooker time

Ingredients:

- 1 cup of sugar, granulated
- 7 & 1/2 cups of milk, 2%
- 3/4 cup of rice, jasmine

Instructions:

1. Rinse rice. Brush a bit of oil inside the bowl of your slow cooker so nothing will stick.

2. Add rice and milk to slow cooker. Cook on high for about three to four hours. Add the sugar during the final hour of cooking. Remove lid. Use wooden spoon to stir. Cover again. Serve.

ooooooooooooooooooooooooooooooooo

28 - Stuffed Figs

This recipe is one of the more traditional ways of cooking figs in Albania, but the recipe does vary from village to village. Some people who make the dish at home don't even use a recipe.

Serving Size: 8 half-servings

Total Cooking Time: 45 minutes

Ingredients:

- 4 figs, fresh
- 8 walnuts, halved
- 5 fluid ounces of water, filtered
- 2 ounces of sugar, granulated

Instructions:

1. Cut off hard parts of the fig stalks. Cut figs lengthwise in half.

2. Place figs in small size fry pan with cut side facing up. Add water.

3. Heat figs on med. heat and cook through. When they're soft, remove from pan. Place on serving dish.

4. Add sugar to red water juice left in pan when you removed figs. Keep it over med. heat. Continuously stir for a few minutes, till juice turns syrupy. Remove it from heat.

5. Push 1/2 walnut in each fig. Drizzle syrup on top. Serve while warm or allow to cool and serve.

oooooooooooooooooooooooooooooooooooo

29 - Albanian Sheqerpare

This is a traditional cookie in Albania and is often served with clear raki brandy or Turkish coffee. This recipe adds a bit of yeast and yogurt and broadens the flavor of the syrup with the use of cloves and orange juice.

Serving Size: 4 Servings

Total Cooking Time: 1 hour & 10 minutes

Ingredients:

- 7 & 3/4 oz. of flour, all-purpose
- 3 & 1/2 oz. of softened butter
- 1 cup sugar, granulated
- 1 large egg, free-range
- 2 tbsp. of plain yogurt, whole fat
- 1 tsp. of yeast
- Pinch of sea salt
- Pistachios, peeled, whole

For syrup

- 7 ounces of sugar, granulated
- 6 & 3/4 fluid oz. of water, filtered
- 1/2 tsp. of orange juice, fresh
- 1/2 tsp. of lemon juice, fresh
- 3/4 tsp. of vanilla extract, pure
- 2 or 3 cloves, whole

Instructions:

1. Preheat the oven to 350F.

2. Cream sugar and butter together in mixer till incorporated fully. Add the egg and combine till you have a smooth mixture.

3. Stir in the yeast, yogurt, salt and flour a bit at a time till it forms a soft dough.

4. On lightly floured cutting board, roll dough out till it is 1/3-inch thick. Cut it into 2" flat circles. Place on cookie sheets lined with baking paper.

5. Press down on dough circles so they will flatten more and show indentations in centers. Place one pistachio nut in middle. Leave some room between cookies, as they'll spread.

6. Put cookies in the oven. Cook for 18-20 minutes, till the cookies are browned lightly.

7. As cookies bake, add water and sugar to small sized sauce pan. Cook on med-high for 12-15 minutes, till syrup spins long, thin thread. Remove it from heat. Season syrup with cloves, vanilla, orange and lemon juices.

8. When the cookies have finished baking, remove them from the oven. Place them on racks to cool down a bit. Pour the syrup over the cookies and serve.

OOOOOOOOOOOOOOOOOOOOOOOOOOOOOOOOOO

30 - Honey Baklava

This type of baklava is created using fresh honey, when available. Many desserts in Albania have a sweet sugary sauce covering them, and some of them substitute honey for that syrup. Allow the honey to soak in well for the best taste.

Serving Size: 15 Servings

Total Cooking Time: 2 hours & 10 minutes

Ingredients:

- 36 sheets of pastry, filo
- 17 & 1/2 oz. of walnuts
- 7 ounces of butter, melted
- 1 tsp. of cinnamon, ground
- 7 & 3/4 oz. of sugar, granulated
- 7 & 1/2 fluid oz. of water, filtered
- 5 & 3/4 oz. of honey, pure

Instructions:

1. To create the syrup, add water, sugar and honey in sauce pan. Stir constantly while bringing to boil.

2. Once sugar melts, leave boiling over med. heat for three to five minutes. Set aside and allow to cool.

3. To create the filling, mix cinnamon and ground walnuts together. Set them aside.

4. Measure ready-made filo dough sheets as compared to the size of the baking tray you will be using. Then cut the pastry to the proper size. Cover with damp towel to keep it moist.

5. Brush some of the melted butter onto sides and base of baking tray. Lay a sheet of the filo pastry one at a time and butter as you lay them. Lay eight sheets. Sprinkle the cinnamon/walnut mixture over pastry.

6. Layer four additional sheets and butter them as you lay them. Add another 1/4 of cinnamon/walnut mixture. Repeat till you have four layers of that mixture.

7. Layer last eight filo sheets, still buttering when laying them. Finish top layer with butter, as well.

8. Baklava can be cut in the way you prefer. Traditionally, it is cut in diamonds.

9. Place baklava in 325F oven. Cook for one and one-quarter hour. After an hour has passed, check the pastry every five minutes. Leave in oven longer if needed. Remove when pastry is crispy and golden.

10. Pour syrup over baklava while it's still hot. The sizzling should be audible. Allow to set out for four hours, so the syrup can soak in through pastry. Serve.

OOOOOOOOOOOOOOOOOOOOOOOOOOOOOOOOOOOO

Conclusion

This Albanian cookbook has shown you...

How to use different ingredients to affect unique middle-eastern tastes in dishes both well-known and rare.

How can you include Albanian cooking in your home recipes? You can...

- Make special midday meals on days when your family will be home. This is the most important meal of the day in Albania. These meals are just as tasty as the ingredients lead you to believe.
- Learn to make salads with many types of vegetables. This is a common way to create salads in Albania.
- Enjoy making the delectable seafood dishes of Albania, including trout, bass and calamari. Fish is a mainstay in the coastal regions.
- Make dishes using beef, lamb, duck and chicken, which are often used in Albanian cooking. There are SO many ways to make them into great meals.

- Make various types of desserts like Albanian Baklava, which will tempt your family's sweet tooth.

Have fun experimenting! Enjoy the results!

ooooooooooooooooooooooooooooooooo

Author's Afterthoughts

Thanks ever so much to each of my cherished readers for investing the time to read this book!

I know you could have picked from many other books, but you chose this one. So, a big thanks for reading all the way to the end. If you enjoyed this book or received value from it, I'd like to ask you for a favor. Please take a few minutes to *post an honest and heartfelt review on Amazon.com.* Your support does make a difference and helps to benefit other people.

Thanks!

Julia Chiles

About the Author

Julia Chiles

(1951-present)

Julia received her culinary degree from Le Counte' School of Culinary Delights in Paris, France. She enjoyed cooking more than any of her former positions. She lived in Montgomery, Alabama most of her life. She married Roger

Chiles and moved with him to Paris as he pursued his career in journalism. During the time she was there, she joined several cooking groups to learn the French cuisine, which inspired her to attend school and become a great chef.

Julia has achieved many awards in the field of food preparation. She has taught at several different culinary schools. She is in high demand on the talk show circulation, sharing her knowledge and recipes. Julia's favorite pastime is learning new ways to cook old dishes.

Julia is now writing cookbooks to add to her long list of achievements. The present one consists of favorite recipes as well as a few culinary delights from other cultures. She expands everyone's expectations on how to achieve wonderful dishes and not spend a lot of money. Julia firmly believes a wonderful dish can be prepare out of common household staples.

If anyone is interested in collecting Julia's cookbooks, check out your local bookstores and online. They are a big seller whatever venue you choose to purchase from.

Printed in Great Britain
by Amazon